Like a Slam

By
Farah Chamari

Table of Contents

Dear reader,

This book has been in the works in its digital form since 2020 and in its paper form since 2016.

The thoughts and poems that made it into this version were specifically selected to match a very infinite number of topics around life, in general.

Although the order is very arbitrary, the choice of making them so is not. The purpose is to highlight to you the contrast between the past and the present and how there's a shift of the mindset, state of mind and the maturity between what was written in the earlier days and what was written in the latest ones.

With that being said, I hope that you would enjoy most, if not all of the passages that made the cut.

My purpose is always the same: sharing stories with the world and going beyond what my comfort zone allows me to.

Sincerely,
Farah Chamari

Beginnings are so sweet.

Oh! how beginnings are so sweet.
You start to think "This might actually be my person", then life
happens, and you end up in the final round of deceit.
How beautiful it is to find that someone with whom you skip the
introductions, and you dive directly into the deep.
You don't get the "nice to meet you", the "where do you live?" and
any question that's too cheap.
You get to open up, be yourself in front of them and think that
they'll appreciate you for who you are... Yet you forget that even
your family members don't get to do that after all... So, why would
a stranger welcome you with open arms?
Well, if we don't get to be fooled by the simple changes in life, you
can't call us humans, right?
We forget that we've been through it before, yet once more, we
lose track, we lose sight.
It might be because of the fact that feelings get involved, or the
fact that by having some faith and trust in others, all of our
problems seem to be solved.
It might be because it's life as we know it, or that we like to seize
every chance rather than simply blow it.
It might be because, with all the tragedies and miseries happening
around us, we would like to hold on every bit of light, rather than
be part of the daily struggles, the daily fights.

21.11.2023

Stuck around.

Life has put in her path chances to test and see who would stick around.
Some excuses were serious, others were trivial.
But no one knew her for who she really was.
They threw away all of her good traits and emphasized on her imperfections.
They walked away thinking that she would be shaken.
They thought it's a way to hurt her, but it was something she didn't care about.
All her life she witnessed several departures, and she never ever considered anyone her partner.
She momentarily filled the voids to make it seem so fun, but nothing was truly felt and that's how things were overly done.
She didn't run after anyone despite being the instigator of any plan.
That's how she was the girl, the woman and sometimes the man.
Her values have no gender, and that's what pushed her to be stronger, and when they ask her if she ever fell in love, not even romantically.
She instantly says "No" and it comes off automatically.
That's her honesty and to her, feelings alternate like a swing.
She can like you during summer then hate you during spring.
It's all about life and its bipolarity by nature,
and you'll keep on seeing the similarities in the future.
Since she'll always be HER no matter what, that's where she belongs, and that is a fact.

27.07.2020

Truth Uncovered

I've finally come to realize your true side.
I instantly knew about it when you lied.
Oh well, you're just one of them, an egocentric type of guy.
I'm sick of the word play, Sick of the tricks.
I'm trying to empower myself a lot.
By empowering others, I got no time to bother.
You decided to ghost me.
But when you got dipped, you got back to texting me,
No! I'm not dumb,
No! I'm not kind.
My ship will never sink again.
My time has come, I've got a new plan.
Act like a kid or like a real man.
Do I seem like I would even care?

18.01.2019

Stuck in Boredom

Living in these lonely days,
While they've gotten their own Baes.
Feeling Pressure, inhaling Routine.
"Things will change!", what do you mean?
Got stuck in this boredom,
pushing me to think we're "an item".
In my head, I've already won Oscars.
A famous actress, one of the big stars.
I played hundreds of shows and dramas,
then reality stroke, that stupid karma!
I tried to survive,
a new atmosphere, I wanted to derive.
It was random, out of the blue.
With this life, what would I do?

One day in 2016.

Seeking Strength

I did not lower my standards.
I knew it when you blew out your chances. Although you could've
had memories to cherish,
you went on being so childish.
You always think that you've got it all.
You were looking up high,
so, watch out that sickening fall.
I don' want to lie,
I might've played it a fool or acted a bit cruel,
but my new adventure has begun,
while our story had reached its end.

Another day in 2016.

Credit to my sixth sense

The only reason I unblocked you is for me not to sound like an immature woman.

I surrendered to my impulsive sentiments, and I acted in the heat of the moment.

I had to undo what I did, not for you, but to make sure that you won't think that you matter that much.

You've seen it before with others, I'm someone who loves to make a fuss about things and I'm still not the one you can easily nudge.

I just express my thoughts in an instant and I don't keep them to myself.

I would lie if I said that I didn't see the signs or if this story didn't ring any bells.

I'm no superwoman. I just fully give credit to my sixth sense.

I felt that it was going to happen that's why I slowly started withdrawing.

Now that I think of it, it wasn't your decision, it was purely my doing.

You know that what I hate the most is people acting up and then coming back as if there was no foul play.

Now I'm not saying that I'm an angel, I've been through that kind of phase as well.

At least I had to clarify my conduct, so we do owe you something to explain.

Before you go on that same narrative and complain, why don't you consider that what you caused is a dissension?

Maybe you were not used to honesty, and you were only exposed to professing...

Seems like I'm not the one that needs to heal if that's even worth mentioning.

For now, I'll stop declaring my issues and I'll only display my best version.

Let's see if that would be appealing enough... I hope you fall for that kind of bluff.

24.11.2023

Shady

They think that they can get through by being shady.
None of them is my spokesperson, they're just jealous of this lady.
Doesn't matter what they say, let them blabber.
Thanks to them, I'm filling up these papers, I'm getting bigger and bigger.
Only empty shells talk bad of you,
even if they laugh, it doesn't mean it's true.
They wanted to trigger the angry birds,
they were aiming at me with their lances,
hoping that I'd be hurt.
Shamelessly portraying it through glances that won't make me intimidated.
These jokes are so outdated.
We're different, we're not mean,
And we're not a group, we're a team.

04.04.2019

Hang in there.

Hang in there, you'll overcome all of the hardships around you.
One day, the clouds will clear, and it will be over.
You will resist it all and be fine.
All will be resolved, one step at a time.
You will happily turn that page.
And you'll shine in your stage.
You are your own star.
You will push your worries very far.
Forget about them, say it every day.
You will rise up and say, Hurray!

19.12.2018

Fake People

Sick of these fake people.
Why Do I have to struggle?
Why should it be a battle?
They tell me, "So, What?",
and I say, I can't deal with people like that.
To them, it sounds very easy.
They tag along in the masquerade, but if I do that, I will fade.
I cannot stand hypocrisy, enjoying ecstasy, living the fantasy.
No, I can't do this. I can't enjoy the bliss,
Insane but... I'd rather throw that fit,
It helps me get better even for a tiny bit.

17.12.2018

Lonely is just a passage.

I hate it so much that I remember everything about you.
Your birthday, your best color, and your favorite TV show too.
I hate it so much that I think of you like we never parted ways, like it's only been days since I saw you by the lake.
When we mocked couples making silly videos in the public eye.
And if I say that I never wanted us to be them, that's my biggest lie.
I hate it that I recall the feelings you convoked in me.
That our memories together didn't dissolve quickly.
They marked their territory in my unforgetting brain.
Making it harder to ease the pain, to break the unlucky chain, like you expect a white clothing to never stain.
Or ride a rollercoaster and never faint.
Or create a bond that would never break.
Or have a friendship that would never shake.
I hate that I still get inspired when it comes to your story.
When you've already moved on and you're not even sorry.
I asked how can someone disappear without a trace?
And that's why they say that you only see the reality when it's shoved in your face.
Why would I blame others for acting like I do?
If all I see is red and what they see is blue?
But it doesn't matter now since everybody else has their own way and I don't like marriage anyway.
I only hate it if I felt lonely. But lonely is selfish. And lonely is just a passage.

21.08.2022

Obsessed

Boy, I swear it's not cute, when you stick around no matter how
hard I pushed you away.
Your words may be sweet,
but I don't feel them, so stop showing up every single day.
Your hysterical obsession is kind of creepy.
I'm not your possession, don't be so weepy.
I said it a million times, there's no "us", So, cut it out!
I'm sick of your infinite chase, it's a bad clout!
Boy, what you do is so cheesy,
how can I wipe my existence from your memory?
How can I block the thoughts you have, those that I don't
understand?
You really need to behave.
Your wishes are just sand.

17.10.2019

The B*'s Comeback

Look, she's here, she has just shown up.
What a strong comeback, she made it at the top.
I tell her every time you won't be able to sustain.
I have been there too, but here I go again.
Naked from the feels, free from the pain.
It's a cycle from which I would like to refrain.
You were not supposed to be viral,
You were meant to make me feel good.
Living with you should be vital.
You won't shake me up, is that understood?
Look, my brain is messed up.
You came to drag me down, But I won't stop.
I have questioned my identity, "she got a rage",
Sinking inside, it's a horrific phase!

One day in 2018.

Last week of July

Coming out to meet you in the middle of the night, is something
I've never done in my whole life.
We enjoyed the breeze and the shining stars.
The moon was full, and I saw the sparkles in your eyes.
We had a deep talk sitting on that old bench.
Embracing feelings, we somehow had to flinch.
You were a bit tipsy which made your cheeks so red.
"Aw he's Cute!": That's what I said in my head.
It was a sweet and romantic movie scene,
When I called you "dude", yet you called me queen.
You know that I captured that moment like a Polaroid picture,
embellished with your eloquent talk that I still hear you whisper.
That last week of July was magical, I won't deny.

28.11.2019

Wish me luck.

Wish me luck, I need to survive this life.
My deep urge to win, but where do I begin?
I wanted everything and all, until I collapse until I fall.
It's a ride or die, a Hi or a goodbye.
Bipolarity got me hard, seems that was all I had.
I needed so much balance, but the weight went up.
I thought there was a chance, but my heart heated up.
Then, my words drew a key, to save it all, to save me.
And my mind flew overseas, to find serenity to find peace.

23.10.2019

Pouring out my heart.

Pouring out my heart has always felt so good, but what makes a difference is when you really listen, dude.
Hearing all my thoughts, being kind and never rude.
Quality time is our number one rule.
I have already been used to the attention.
I love that laughing is your ultimate reaction, and for that I would love to mention that I like deep, but I also like the funny, because we may have clouds, but we also face the sunny. Which is a great metaphor to describe the person you are.
I know that you've got your darker sides, like everyone else, but what matters is that your cheerful one overshadows it by far.
You said you'll love it if someone wrote something for you and I'm really glad that my inspiration of today is you.
Although you're too cringy for my liking, your vibe just lifts up the mood, just like a walk, just like a hiking.
Caring and paying attention to the slightest details, that, my friend, is a recipe that never fails.
Keep being the authentic person you truly are, and you'll shine brighter than the stars.
Moral of the story is, being around the right people brings the best in us,
and to me, that's the secret to relationships that last.

18.09.2023

It's hard.

I can tell that it's hard with all these girls stacked up by your side.
My inner charms, that's my hidden card.
No worries, I got nothing to hide.
No hurries, I'm sure that one day you'll see the tide.
But now, you see them in different sorts.
You see the appetizers while I can give you comfort.
Be your human tranquilizer loving the physical stuff.
That's not eternal, especially not when things get a little tough.

28.01.2019

Anxiety

Doing this kind of business gave me anxiety.
How many years am I going to miss?
And pursue with this mentality?
The bad reality.
My brain deserves equity.
A little bit of sanity.
Not afraid of dynasty.
Even if we lose faith in humanity.
I have got to treat insomnia,
So, I'm fine if I sipped some mania.

12.04.2019

Sweet words

You confuse me with the sweet words that feel like song lyrics.
You sure know how to make the jaws drop.
You have got some witty tactics.
You don't know what you want,
Yet all you do is flaunt.
I know, it sounds like I'm bashing you.
I'm not even blaming you.
Surely, I'm not willing to let you break me one more time.
I'm all good, Thanks! I'm fine!
I know you're eloquent.
In romance, you're never reluctant.
But maybe, you should think it through.
This time, it won't be easy to step in, but let's see where this is going...

10.01.2019

The scent of the neighborhood

Cute little girl sitting in the window calling my name.
Two beautiful souls trying hard to get to staying the same.
Her mama's delicious food,
The memories of our childhood.
The scent of the neighborhood.
The folks that were so good.
The magical relationships.
Eternal friendships.

12.02.2019

Darkest shade of red

I didn't need to hear the words from you to believe in what's so true.

I didn't need to hear them in a spoken form since that's what my brain tells me, ever since I was born.

Maybe the reasons changed but we can't skip the fact of who is it about.

I'm complicated, I'm not a green or even a gray flag... I'm probably the darkest shade of red that has ever existed in this world.

I admit that things can get confusing and that it's not a given for anyone to handle me.

Let's be honest here, I get extremely annoyed, and I escape whenever I see another version of me.

So, I can't be judgmental about it when the roles are reversed. But I also can't help but think that this repeated pattern makes me feel like I'm cursed.

Or maybe the idea itself is reassuring as I won't be the problem here.

I know that I may have contributed to it, but I refuse to be the sole responsible for the outcomes of every relationship that slips away from me....

If I consider my age, the number of people who I lost touch with is not that big of a deal. Evidently, it's the same way with everybody else, or at least it's how I see it or how I feel.

I won't deny that I attempted to change the direction every time, but I failed miserably at it. Because whenever my logic got awakened, it was almost too late to revoke what was built, what was shared and what was taken.

I don't get to fully give away my trust, but damn man, if I cared for you, it's like that 1% that's left to fully make you land on my safe list.
But I've got to give it to you though: Talking night and day, showing you that I care, acting like you're the most important one and including you in every plan, giving nicknames and being cheeky despite it not being in my nature, probably making you question on whether my statements are legit or just for pretend...
All of this is real, and I understand why you might be addled, but I've always been clear about who I am, how my statements are not theoretical, and that I fully stand by what I defend.
That if I repeat myself a lot, it's to make sure that you don't assimilate things otherwise.
That you should take what I say as a literal meaning and not as a twisted line.
That's the least to do with a very direct person: no need to analyze any words or behavior.
If I still don't comprehend certain things about me, don't try to be my savior.
So, here's my very serious question: am I really the bad guy? or did my sincere demeanor look like a lie?
Is it really me the one to blame? or does any uncontrolled emotion the reason for the downfall? That's quite a shame... There would be no point behind our history,
or maybe there was regardless of it being a defeat or a victory.
Unfortunately, every start has its own end, and so far, my endings are simply losing games.

22.11.2023

Creepy

I mean this life's a creepy place.
Backstab me and then smile to my face.
Yes, that's another phase.
Yes, our world's a maze.
Run away from the blaze.
I bet kindness' just a craze.
I mean this life made me dwell.
Doesn't matter if you screw up or do well,
because your road can be blocked.
The luck is under lock.
Hate to be stuck in this circle?
Would you rather be a fickle?

11.09.2019

Not sure

Not sure if I can take it any longer.
I need a cure to my problems; they're getting bigger and bigger.
What to endure, I'm growing sicker and sicker.
Trying to lure: The load wouldn't be thicker.
It's a whole cloud up there.
This is why I probably wanted to share.
reduce its huge size.
Don't complain or criticize,
when it's already a crisis,
And life is never a fair game.
You only pass the test when you're lame,
but I never belonged to these shows,
and because of that I had to suffer thousands of blows.

Another day in 2019.

Sassy

I say all I want; you may think it's sassy.
The way I move, I sit, I dress, it's classy.
No need for the colors to be flashy.
You'll just notice me super quick; I know I'm catchy.
Because when I'm sly,
you'll just fly.
My rhythms are poppy and blues.
I've got no time for these dudes.
All I want is a hippy dance.
All I want is to be happy.
All you need is a glance,
to forget what crappy is!

03.04.2019

The angle

If people had a close look at it, they would notice that it was all
about the angle.
Despite the messy circumstances of this jungle, I'm not a looped
rankle.
Regardless of my many bungles, I knew exactly how to handle all
of the haggles.
Not to mention the struggles that made me shamble, or the
mantles that made me thankful.
See? Told you it was all about the angle.
Other than those with whom I shared a blood, or the one behind
my whole existence, the
Almighty God.
The remaining part said that I was " a lot", and that it was such a
heavy plate that I got.
Or they actually had nothing to express,
the silence said all the words they suppressed.
So, my actions continued to protest, and then I decided to be
repressed.
To find other ways to remove it out my chest, So, I laughed, sang,
and danced,
and reminded myself of the words stuck on my wall.
the double "L"s that sums it all,
You put them there for your eyes to see,
and to remind you of the meaning behind putting them
back-to-back because they're so entwined.

14.09.2020

Tell me

Tell me what you really want now.
All you do is blame me, about the "what?" and "how?".
I'm not complaining, you know me too well.
Why don't you say it or send your farewell?
I'm done with these tricks,
the playing with the chicks.
Hard heart as bricks.
Throwing the flicks.
Saying it's complicated,
Getting me all twisted,
No debate here.
Everything is pretty clear.
And another day in 2019 in class.

Gorgeous

Lifting you up was a no-brainer.
That's how we rule, by empowering each other.
Gorgeous, you should learn it on your own.
Your greatness is what we've always known.
Do it right, don't stay out of sight.
You shine so bright,
Make these standards so tight.
Down to earth yet you value your worth.
No back and forth,
It's a south or a north.
With a full glam on,
You're so prestigious,
You're a swan.

16.02.2020

Drafting the empty time

Could you tell me what was the trigger?
To mess up with me and make me hear your snigger?
I thought that you were my kind of balladist.
You turned out to be such a sadist.
I'm someone that did never flinch, but with you I craved for a
clinch.
You were an equivalent of security when I pictured us together for
an eternity...

17.04.2019

Mother

You gave birth to me, yet it feels like we're unrelated and then you
see, it makes me quite disgusted.
Every now and then a new thing pops up again.
We're sick of the ideas you always defend.
They say blood is thicker than water,
but why I am so ashamed to call you mother.
It's absurd that I have part of your DNA,
it's absurd that I have to act like it's ok.
It saddens me that I hold all this grudge on the inside,
because I know that one day, you'd no longer be by our side.
I can't help but think of that moment to face, nothing but
frustration and hate filling up the space.
Hundred deeds won't make it for your wrongdoings; can't you get
it already through your shortcomings?
Mother, why can't you be mature?
Mother, can I call you that anymore?

07.12.2019

No

No, I don't need a backup.
Don't need that to lift myself up.
Putting more fuel on this.
It's not a rap battle, It's not a diss.
You're not cynical,
put that brain to rest.
This is so critical,
you need a clinical test.
"No pain, no gain",
but it's the same anyway.

Again, 2019.

What's wrong with me?

I'm wondering what's wrong with me?
Waking up in the middle of the night.
Struggling to shut my own mind up.
Looking for the person that I used to be.
Stressing out, shouting out to my own self.
I want to break free; I want to survive.
Bottled up, I should've packed my worries on the shelf.
I need to snuggle; I need to thrive.
I'm wondering what's wrong with me.
I would love to get my act together.
I want to have that peace, my glee.
Praying for days to get better, while trusting that this won't last
forever.

End of 2018.

Vivid memories

Vivid memories, I have of you.
I still see you, reminisce about you.
Vivid memories, I see as true.
Bringing up the nostalgy that you were my Boo.
How come we don't exist anymore.
We were the happiest, I'm sure.
Our love was pure, was hardcore.
I thought that I was the one you have been looking for.
Now we're torn apart... you broke my heart.
It has been so dark, I've flunked.
Should've known better when you were always drunk.
Vivid memories, I have to get out of my head.
I had to bring back the sleep when I go to bed.
Vivid memories, I see as true, but you're no longer my Boo.

31.10.2018

Sunshine to snow

Moving from sunshine to snow.
Why can't you let me know?
How did we reach this?
How can I understand this?
You left me in the dark side.
Your love for me was never that wide.
It hurts to state the facts, because of your contradictory acts.
It became weighing down on me.
Could not wrap my head around it.
I'm aware that I should let it be,
I know it's hard, but I had to face it.
An embarked disaster,
I wish I could heal faster.
No options to choose.
It's an "I win, or I lose".

Someday in 2018.

Me

Your perception may tell you that I'm oppressed and not
empowered.
You'll find it hard to believe that a girl like me is pretty tolerant
and open-minded.
Because when you get to know the real me, you'll switch off your
judgmental opinions.
What the media had fed you is nothing but fake so stop being
their minions.
Yes, you can see me in the clubs enjoying explicit songs.
Yes, you can get me wrong while I'm giving away hugs.
Yet I'm conservative in a world where everything is allowed, and
my purpose in life isn't about following the crowd. What you
think is freedom is not to me,
what you think is wisdom, there's no wisdom I see.
Why don't you live your life without a tease?
Can't I just live it the way I please?
Why are you complaining about me be being different?
Why should I be explaining the meaning of the non-prominent?
Are they happy for having a loveless intercourse?
What's there to brag when they're so depressed, of course!
Get all wasted and fainting in streets,
zombies roaming around shouting in screams, with sad eyes and
hopeless souls,
even with hundreds of bucks and millions of jewels.
If that's bringing out the card of "YOLO",
I'd rather be in my exceptional mind all being solo!

01.05.2019

Covid-19

We were caught off guard while we were busy complaining about
our lives.
So, the monster came and took it all from us : we started waking
up on the news of a deadly virus.
Everything was put to a halt.
It suddenly became everyone's fault.
Then we were confined, forced to a lockdown.
But in a blink of an eye, numbers exceeded half a million.
Even the weather had the time to revenge, so, we were left with
nothing but cringe.
Haunted by a fear of a positive testing,
that would wipe out everything that counts as a blessing.
The Inner cleanliness maniacs kicked in.
Anything from outside had to be questioned.
Staying home was the only medicine,
and if you go out? You're committing a big sin.
Wuhan, where it all began,
You screwed up bitch, you killed all the fun.
We wonder when we will stop the isolation.
When will this quarantine thing come to a termination?
Can we ever stop the spread?
Can we really prevent others from being dead?

27.03.2020

Why?

Everybody's asking me why?
I'm so delighted when I see your eyes.
But babe, you get me cringe out of fear.
But why are you never clear?
You told me that I'm the best and that you want to break the ice.
Then, spill your guts, and tell me the words... that are nice.
Got me spinning in a circle,
you put me in a daze.
I was wishing for a miracle,
but this road is just a maze.
Because everybody's asking me why,
My attachment to you is something I can't deny.
I now should seek protection.
I'd better get out of this list of "perfection".

Some Time in 2017.

Emotions

From these emotions I got a strike.
Nothing is satisfying me; it all seems fake.
Don't want to remain in the low, I'd better reach that height. I'm
bearing with what it actually takes,
but what if I hate to procrastinate?
Maybe it requires creativity, or a little more sensitivity.
You should know the poverty to enjoy the royalty and get defeated
by these slaps of cruelty.
No, I don't want to live these bits.
I've got my share of these hits; does it really need drama to have
the power?
Does it really take effort to oust tower?
Can't we have some peace for that human skull?
Can't we prevent it from taking a toll?
I said it once and I'll say it again, this is not for me; I despise this
domain.

03.04.2019

So. Gu. So Dull.

I came into your life when you needed an emotional support,
and you came into mine when I was just simply bored.
I wanted to believe the astrology folks,
that told me we're compatible,
but we're just a goat and a bull,
an item you say? that's just so dull.
You appeared at the right time and also left at the right one.
God knows better, and that's the reason things just happen.
It was cool dude! you made me test my patience level.
You gave me some anecdotes to tell,
and you showed me once more that my list is not a detail,
that it's so important to stick to it or things are bound to fail.
But what I'm most proud of is how I prioritized myself love,
and that I put nothing else above.
That I was this great wave of positive energy.
That I kept my composure with situations that would normally get
the best of me,
That I was sharing wisdom with people who are passing by,
and I said this because it was a super rapid goodbye.
Oh! you thought it's hard for me to ditch you out of my life, with
zero memories or any good thing to hold on to other than wasted
time?
I knew it since day one that you're everything I hated in people.
I was no longer fine with mysteries,
or the twisted sentences.
The intolerance and narrow-mindedness,
or the cultural and social gaps,

and the inferiority complex, that's a lot!
But to make this fair, it's nice to hear sweet words even if I
believed none,
and your voice was hot on the phone,
and the attention you wanted to give; it was alright but never
enough.
You were pretty cute in pictures, that's a fact.
I know it takes a lot for people to change for the better, but I
honestly wish you'd fulfill your dreams and you'd become more
stable.
That you'd find your person, the one who "will understand",
because this short fling of ours is seasonal,
and if you ever read this, don't think of it as special.
It's just my way of finishing business in the most artistic way.
That's what my poetry book is about, that's what statistics say.

02.07.2021

Got it?

There are days when you get excited; Your heart is shivering and so
is your soul.
You do whatever it takes to reach your goal.
Pressured by deadlines, you wish your time would get extended.
Never let go of what you got. You might want to give in .
Eventually, you will not.
Whether you get bullied, teased, or even shot.
Skip that chapter, fill your life with laughter.
You wouldn't even remember how it all went.
If they tried to make you fail, but they simply can't.
It's what I exactly meant, this blessed moment.
Kill them with a bright smile.
That would be spotted from a mile.
I have gotten no worries anymore.
Sadness? I already shut that door.

A random day in 2017.

A birthday wish

Happy Birthday to my only one.
Hope that nothing will come undone.
That you'd enjoy yourself more and have some extra fun.
That your worries and hardships will be forever gone.
That your this birthday will be a very blessed one.
That you'll get untangled from whatever is bringing you down.
That you'll forever be surrounded by your loved folks.
That you'd have a blast even from small walks.
That you'd meet your soulmate, a person who's not shallow.
The one for which your heart will beat and entirely fall for.
This may not be your first customized letter,
But I'm confident enough to say that you won't find better.
You know!, not anyone is born to be a poet or a writer.
I simply hope that I could warm your heart up in this cold winter.
Wish you some extravagantly joyful days,
and that the hidden best moments can finally find their ways.
From this foreign figure,
to the person who has just gotten bigger.

02.02.2019

Wrecked world

Look at how the world is functioning now.
Seems like the war has made a vow,
to push it all to vanish, filling it with blemish,
blood stains are all over the floors, global warming knocked the
doors.
Innocent smiles have never seen the light, they had a magical
energy to ignite, should've let them go to schools,
but you went on laughing in your castles taking us as fools.
While your kids are swimming in the big pools, you're monitoring
others' lives like widget tools.
Bloody monsters ruling the planet, moody fuckers, spreading the
hate.
Blaming it on religions, those real terrorists.
Shutting up opinions, killing the artists.
Reflecting virtual pictures in the media, spitting your own info
like encyclopedia.
When is this going to end? when is this going to mend? shall we
carry on in our blindness?
Shall we witness the upcoming darkness?

23.04.2019

Blemishes

You barged into my life without a consent,
then you cut me off like a sharp knife.
Tore me apart, is that what you wanted? To put me in ashes!
I gave you attention, I guess you've been granted some wishes.
It's all I had anyways,
I know about my blemishes, but I showed none to you regardless,
Oh! hold on... Wait!
Did you believe that nonsense?
I give no jacks about your betrayal!
I don't live the fake fairy tales.

A 0-inspiration day in 2017.

Rom-Com

Everybody's wishing for their romantic comedy.
Everybody's wanting to get a soulful remedy.
Someone who'd spawn food for thought.
Someone who isn't slick to share a serious talk.
Some precious moments that make their hearts beat.
Valuable Emotions hanging on fleek.
Getting tired of the "situationships".
Craving for authentic relationships.
Don't want the money, just nice cribs.
Don't want the honey, just sweet dips.

14.11.2019

Social retirement

I've always found a sense of relief when I spoke out.
I claim a high level of integrity that I'm so proud of.
Though that road doesn't ensure a place in this society,
I tend to go for it even after suppressing it wholeheartedly.
I realize that truth is always ugly and unwelcomed,
but a repressed brain can get deeply overwhelmed.
And because I don't want to sail in a sinking ship,
I hold firmly into my values and take a grip.
Then, I find it refreshing to go against people's grains,
to be the courageous person that fears nothing when it comes to
the right thing.
It's somehow sad that honesty leads to a bad reputation.
While bystanders love the play and show me ovation, the claps in
the background celebrate my social retirement,
and I play the fool but I understand the full agreement:
" There's no room for sincere thoughts,
there's no space for any type of defense.
So, if you still want to use your shots,
your social existence will be forever dispensed".

15.12.2020

No Need

Not asking you to understand, in all cases all I do is pretend.
These crazy values I defend, don't need any hands to be tended.
I'm not faking, I'm really aching.
These mental issues made me waste a bunch of tissues. Take a
breath, let it all out.
As long as it isn't death, don't freak out.
This is what I try to say, every single day.
This routine dived deep into my skin, can't figure out from where
to begin,
bottled up from letting it all in.
I'm trying to see all what matters, what's within.
Screw it all, I should be crashing it.
This mess needs to stop,
Screw it all, I'll get back to my real spot, let's bring back that
period that dot.

03.04.2019

Unexpected departure

I can't even picture leaving you behind,
that thought alone kills me inside.
All I can think of is how it'd tear you apart,
how it'd devastate you and break your heart.
You're the kind that sobs over anyone's misfortune,
so, what would you do if we left a little too soon?
How can your tiny soul handle the weight of that unavoidable
departure?
I'm afraid that it'd stop you from continuing your own adventure.
I want you to keep on being a queen,
be always proud of who you are and who you've always been, of
the small things that you could achieve.
Long they were, or even if they're too brief,
but most of all, don't continue the grief.
Because we'll join forces again,
not on earth but probably in heaven.
So, carry on our legacy,
Do it, just do it for me.

21.07.2020

Lifespan

Looking back at the past and I'm so shook.
Deserting everybody, that's all it took.
I still don't know if I'm wrong or they are.
Maybe because I'm too strong, I mean... so far.
When I gave them the moon, but they were reaching out for the
stars.
Nothing but painful memories, nothing but the scars.
I know we need networking to make it in this planet,
but having fake and shallow people is not my kind of mindset.
What do I get? other than being upset?
How do I forget, all the bad words they said?
I don't know my lifespan,
but I'll fight as long as I can.

08.12.2019

Not good at PDA

Baby I'm no good the PDA.
Maybe She's so good, she's good at her own way.
It's your life to choose if you'd leave her or you'd stay.
At the end, I'll be your only bae.
Keeping her by your side : romantic mogul vibe,
dancing on Señorita,
leaving me all Solita.
She'll be your next ex,
backlashing with ghosted texts.
Proving to you that it's me,
roam around but it's where you should be.

28.08.2019

Humble

So great to be humble, no need to mention the struggle.
We've all seen it before; you're just spending it in the stores. Live
simply and enjoy the real things.
a small meal or Ariana's 7 rings.
A laughter with friends eating sweets,
oh wait! you'd rather take empty pics in the streets.
If having fancy stuff made them happy,
you wouldn't see those riches getting sloppy.
Living life isn't about splurging.
So annoying to see you diverging.
I mean, no grudges here, getting slapped at once, that's what I fear.
Life gets tough sometimes, you know.
Want to learn it the hard way to actually grow?
hoping that you'll wake up from the fairy tale,
one day or another you'll go down the scale.
Sorry that you'll ignore these pieces of advice,
you're too arrogant to know that we're just being nice.

21.04.2019

Hospital's bed

Laying in the hospital's bed,
while you were caressing my swallowed hand.
You didn't care about anyone else,
even if my parents were there,
you still didn't care.
You showed up every single time,
gifting me with your priceless presence,
looking at me with your emerald, green eyes,
and the silly me said that you were just being nice.
You spoke love through actions,
and I only gave you bland reactions.
I still recall taking that third shot,
you could've been sick of it, but you were not.
You stuck around until the last second of the visiting hours. In a
glimpse of a sleep, I saw you sitting in the room's corner.
Your silence spoke a billion words,
you still came when I needed you most,
when I was okay and when I was lost.
Now I can only give you my thoughts,
but I still want to reach out sometimes,
for the sake of us, for the sake of the old times.

14.01.2021

Sky's clearer

While my sky's clearer than it used to be, I could still see some
passing clouds here and there: Some of them tend to be lightly
gray, others are dark so often.
It's like the regular spring days: Just because the sun is up, it doesn't
mean that it's that hot. Just because the sky is blue, it doesn't mean
that it's not cold out there.
That's exactly how my world functions... You get to see the
happiest life-coach in the entire world today and the most
pessimistic and saddest person the following day.
Reminders of how easily forgettable I am. Constant proofs on
how insanely replaceable we are.
Unnecessary thoughts of loneliness and missed shots of happiness.
It's like everyone else is rotating while I'm staying still. It's like I
always have another useless time to kill.

09.04.2022

A little something

A year back in time, we got back in touch again.
I don't know what it is about you that made me feel something.
I was brutally happy yet anxious, since it was always fishy and
suspicious.
These opposite shades you had, got me all worked up, all mad, and
since you were into the kind that's feminine, while I know I'm not.
"It would succeed when you're genuine", it's what I actually
thought. I said that I'm not a delusional dreamer, but I had faith in
what is untrue.
Since I'm a hardcore believer, I wanted my fate to be you. what are
the odds of me falling for someone who's far from being my type?
or did the attraction laws hide from me a special one who would
join the hype? Now that my poems rhyme, I would love to say
sweet things.
Even if we lost touch again, whatever happens, happens.

25.11.2019

Enchanted

I see you tasting all that poisonous candy, seems delicious isn't? I
mean, maybe?
I'm familiar with all of that, I'm living in the same world anyway,
but why does it feel insane watching you go out of your way.
You're not the little innocent kid I called my friend, but when
you'd need it tended, I'd still give you my hand.
Telling you: my love can easily turn into hate,
you already know it, that's not a debate.
I loathe this state so horribly, you don't care about it, probably.
Can't blame you for being enchanted by your identical peeps,
though you used to be skeptical about your values and your deeds.
And I've always wanted you to lighten up, never be shocked of
what's there.
I never thought that when I wake up, you'd display your garbage
everywhere. We all have different hidden sides, that's for sure.
and we'd be smitten by those new rides, that are so impure.
It disheartens me to give you my usual advice and wisdom.
Since we see in opposite directions, I lost my chance, oh damn!
So dear Old BFF, I despise your fade-out.
You're at the top of a cliff, it's stressing me out. Nevertheless, you're
an adult now.
Thus, I'd care less. I'm breaking our old vow.
You know it's different when I'm writing this down.
I could just tell you this while you're still in the town.
However, I can't, my friend, you won't even be listening because
you're enchanted by your friends, so I'm just surrendering.

14.11.2019

Rush

I tend to rush things and get them done all at once.
Then I pay for the consequences, the good and the bad ones.
I tell myself each time, take it easy take it slow.
But I follow the same path once more, I follow the same flow.
My sense of authority and obsessive control,
let's just chill and forget about it all.
Because when you rush it, you crush it.
So, let me smash it down the road to success.
There is nothing to fear less than a life we're aiming to possess,
or people we're hoping to impress.

19.12.2019

Branded

While they branded me as a bad girl, I changed my plan, I had to
swirl. I showed them reactions they didn't expect. I gave them
some hard thoughts to collect. Made them wonder what to say
next, and I did what I evaluated as best.
To me, this is a form of mental dysmorphia.
Juggling in the land of fierce Zootopia.
I've been roaming around the same area.
Shifting from deep depression to mania,
and ditching is forever my plan, though I wish that I'd one day be a
stan.
That I'd stay no matter how strong is the storm,
that I'd disregard my ego and follow the norm,
yet, it doesn't feel right when I get frustrated,
so I trust my gut again, until this whole mess is alleviated.

20.11.2020

Do you?

Do you feel what I'm feeling right now?
Do you want to figure it out, but you don't know how?
Is your road as foggy as mine?
Do you sense some chills down your spine?
Are you trying not to let yourself down?
but still want to sit on the crown?
Am I the only one who's confused about their entire existence?
and I can't seem to win over my spooky silence?
Horrifying wakeup calls: the type that alerts.
Petrifying stares at walls, that really hurts.
Endless efforts to tidy things up in here.
Countless actions going against my fear.
I'm like an Alzheimer patient in their final stages : nothing but
dead glares in infinite phases,
What else is there to face? What else is there to ace?
This augmented reality is nothing but deteriorating.
Is it life or death that we're demonstrating?

19.12.2019

New Rhyme

Something about this makes me wonder.
If this is real love, then I shouldn't suffer.
You left a mark in me, a kind of stamp,
every time I forgive you, I feel like a dumb.
My efforts are being wasted,
you're the one I shouldn't have dated,
but this thing in my chest, is reminding of my past.
The moments of sweet feelings,
silly ones with no deep meanings, and I want to leave it to the
time.
Worst case scenario, it'll be my new rhyme.
Something about this makes me stronger.
If it isn't strength, then how did I conquer.
You grew something in me, a kind of a glam.
I will never forgive you, that's a hard bam.
My efforts are being cherished,
my love for you has just perished.
And this thing in my chest,
made of me one of the best.

19.04.2019

Grateful

When the car was skidding and me and my friends went out ok,
I mean who are you kidding,
this is enough reason to go and pray.
When the cancer got smashed, all of the fears were crashed, and
the pain went away.
To God I'm very grateful.
To his grace I'm more than thankful.
When I was drifting apart, and aching was breaking my heart.
When I was crumbling down, and there was no light, no sunshine.
He led me to that path, the bright one.
My belief, my faith, this is what should be done.
To God I'm grateful,
to his grace I'm more than thankful.

03.04.2019

April

Reading my own words, I want to recall what happened last April.
I figured out that, once again, I was just a pupil. I meant in life, not at work or at school.
I was trapped once more; I was such a fool.
I don't know if I was too dramatic, or if my experiences were passively traumatic.
Since I was having a sort of a concussion, everything pushed me to revulsion.
I looked through my lyrics aiming to decode the message, but my memory failed me.
Is it fortunate though, that I didn't document that journey? I didn't explicitly state what bothered me and I chose to leave it hanging in the unknown space.
In an attempt to be wise, I had to be reminded that even if it was too much to handle,
"Look at the surprise, you ended up forgetting about that in no time. You moved past it; you overcame that shit".

09.02.2020

My love life

One, he said he loved me, but he was done, left it all behind and
he just ran.
Seems like it was all for fun, not sure if he lost or won.
So, I was off to the second one,
who barely knew me, but he said he loved me all along.
That he sees me more than a friend, but it was hard for me, so it
had to end.
He was a good guy, and he was so kind,
Not my type though so I can't pretend.
Then I was off to another one, who was so gentle but who I had to
friendzone.
Way out of his league so I'm not what he could own.
But I told him all about it, that I had to warn,
"don't love me man!", don't call me on my phone.
and he got all obsessed, so I was off to another one.
Who was a foreigner that I named Wan, I saw potential but there
was none.
In a blink of an eye, he was already gone. Matter of a fact, it made
me all so hone.

28.11.2019

Guess who's Back?

I'm seeing changes all over my body, while my reflection asks,
"who's that buddy?"
I'm doing it purposely to free my mind from overthinking.
That's supposedly going to save me from sinking.
I burst a toxic bubble, I put myself in trouble.
When I forced perfection into every corner of my life,
I saw that satisfaction is for my mind to have.
He tricked me to focus on every blemish,
but I had tons of things that I could cherish, I had it all, yet I was
depressed,
could've been happy and all but I was distressed.
So, I caressed my pains and switched the direction.
I let go of everything that sounded like a deceiving addiction.
I gave time to myself to mend and heal, that's my journey that I
want to steal,
I claimed back my Joyful laughter and smile, I'll fight against my
fictional hormones for a while.
I'm a strong woman that made a comeback, in that cycle, I'll never
be stuck.

27.12.2019

Time Machine

I wish that we could access a time machine,
I just want to be twelve all over again.
I was the happiest back then,
Null worries... Oh I miss it.
but it's life... Let's just face it.
Mate... I feel very rejected by everybody,
I know it's fate, to be disconnected: soul and body.
Dizzy all the time, I can't think of the how and why.
Phased in my mind, I'm even wishing to die.
These aren't suicidal thoughts,
they're just survival thoughts.
When I read this year's resolutions,
I have barely a month left to make revolutions.
Tell me if you have a way, if you have solutions.
I'm getting the hell out of here: to where, you ask me?
Oh, I'll just follow my intuitions, my guts are strong enough, trust
me, I'll find out how to finish my tuitions. For now, I need peace, I
need revival, I'll just go, I don't need anyone's approval.

14.11.2019

My worth

You contacted me thinking that I was the average type.
I just followed along; I just followed the hype.
I proved myself through experience and through my intellect.
But you're here to get cheap ends, you've only got money to
collect.
I'm a woman who knows her worth, I know exactly what I deserve.
One thing for sure, is that I won't bend to your dirty curve.
I won't obey your ridiculous rule, I won't let you take me for a fool.
I was born in a country that belittles potential resources who work
hard,
and maybe you thought that I was desperate right from the start,
Trust me people... I'm definitely not.
I just had it in my guts, I knew that I was going to get through and
that it will eventually fall apart.
I will never sell my soul; I will never give away my heart.
You're free to think that I'm arrogant, or to think that I missed
out.
I, for sure, didn't, it's simply your own loss.
To say that ethnicity and race are not involved in your decisions is
a non-cynical lie.
You can still toss your own offer into the trash,
I still got things to achieve, I still got things to smash.

20.02.2023

Without a proper goodbye

Feels like a life sentence, spending it under the creepy walls of a
prison.
Feels like we're being punished for the crime of simply living.
It's too hard to swallow,
It's too tough to be mellow.
People are gone without a proper goodbye.
They were all alone, and it hurts to not even try.

28.03.2020

Rocking diss

Lately, my records are quite rocking.
Actually, a diss is often so shocking.
But what if I wanted to spill the tea?
Freedom of expression, Oh Gee!
The cells in my head love to gossip.
who am I to block that zip?
I'm not even capable of that, so, I just chill and join the chat.
I don't always like it but, going against them, I'm a scaredy cat.
So, what's wrong with that?
Don't try and play it the bat.
remember why I wrote this in the first place.
Clearing the air for the sake of my own pace.
I'm not pretentious, I'm well down to earth.
You see it as overconfidence, I see it as knowing my worth.
This is not a battlefield,
and I'm not willing to yield.
You just need to recognize my honesty,
shaping words beautifully is not my specialty.
I'm trying to improve as it put me in trouble,
It won't happen that soon, sorry for bursting your bubble.

23.04.2019

No Taste

My life has actually no taste.
When I thought that I did what it's best,
it made no sense whatsoever,
and it didn't get any better.
Feeling like a loser, it sucks.
I don't care about these few bucks,
as long as my body's with no soul.
I feel like a drop in a swimming pool.
I barely laugh nowadays.
I barely smile, it's such a waste.
What to be happy for when life has no meaning.
Well, I don't feel like I've touched the ceiling,
I can't be glad about what I have,
you'd notice it easily reading the above,
but living with this is truly tough,
this is not nonsense, not a bluff.
It's the only time both my heart and mind align,
maybe it's another instigating sign.
That I should leave it all behind,
start from zero, be a famous weirdo.
Heavy weight that I carry,
wishing that I'd be saved by a fairy.
I have no positive thoughts, I'm so sorry.
Redeem my cheerful side back, that's my goal now.
Wish me some luck, to finally blow.

17.09.2019

Thrift a heart

You had every reason to drift apart, as I made it look like I'm the type who would thrift a heart.
Notwithstanding the fact that I was very transparent from the start, you were right when you stated that it's not evident to manage the situation, to push yourself not to depart...
I was genuine about you and as I knew that we were sitting on the tip of the iceberg, I made sure to document everything we lived together, so that when I reach a day like today, you would still be a person of whom I was fond.
From what I stand, the problem was you listening but not actively doing so. Like you would express your appreciation of anything when you actually don't.
You never spoke your true mind with me and that made me believe that we were on the same wavelength.
You always stated that my honesty is not a flaw rather than a strength.
Until the day I was stabbed in the back. When you said that you understood my point and I was right, then you switched the speech a minute later... which left me in tears, left me in a wreck.
The crying wasn't the worst part, what was is you never regretting acting like that.
Then discrediting everything I said, and discouraging every attempt I made to reach what I pictured as success.
It might not be personal, as this is how you act even with yourself...
Pronouncing pessimistic words while your alter ego was preserved as your inner voice.

Whilst when you needed a hand, I was there to support, to rejoice.
Showing my content about things that helped you thrive but all I got was competitive feedback from your end.
It bothers me that it came from a person I saw as a soulmate, as a friend.
It was another way to finally leave the temporary dreamland.
We're still in touch and you might wonder why I'm showing you different behaviors.
Sometimes I'm nice and very talkative, while other times, I repulse, step back and our interactions become fader and fader.
It's because I stop when the conversation would bring me to hate you, or if it would set off my defensive side, maybe my angry side too.

25.11.2023

Detectives

When they all become detectives,
making me look like a liar.
I don't know what're their incentives.
Watch me, here's my alibi.
Conspiring against me, stirring the public.
They have to stop it; this is so chronic.
They are speaking with confidence,
turning lives, a bit intense.
Proving my innocence, switching on my defense.
Excuse me but no offense,
"Would you speak with more sense?
I don't get your kind of intolerance".

12.01.2020

Change

Constantly looking for a new thing,
something to discover, something to change.
A new adventure, a new thrilling challenge.
That thing that won't make me binge or cringe,
I easily get bored, I admit.
It may be a little hard for me to commit,
a sick perfectionist,
or maybe a revolutionary artist, or is that OCD?
Should I really worry?
All these messy thoughts I carry,
I only found anxiety to marry.
I swear, I shouldn't care to let it all go, I should dare.
A fair play that is, probably born to make these words not babies.
I'm not getting sensitive out here, I'm just stating facts, what's
actually real.

02.04.2019

Tiny things

Even the tiny things matter,
A long walk or a quick chatter.
what did I want better, than these memories I gathered?
These feelings I swallowed.
These emotions I followed.
A happy life is self-made, look at everything you did. That's all I
hear from people nowadays,
I tried to believe it in multiple ways.
But I guess living the Earth theme isn't really for me yet.
Still searching the props but I think it's sought in a different
planet, and I know, I'll get through this one day, perhaps.
I'd try to suffocate the negativity in me, so I won't collapse.
Who am I convincing here? Am I throwing excuses out of fear?

04.11.2019

I hate.

I hate the lies and having to compromise.
I hate hypocrisy and an irrational policy.
I hate looking for a purpose and dealing with non-sense.
I hate feeling useless and finding no words to express.
I hate being misunderstood and always meeting the wrong dude.
I hate the loneliness and the urge to attain happiness.
I hate the arrogance and the obligation to seek defense.
I hate being stressed out and ultimately reaching a burnout.
I hate hearing about violence or anything that's intense.
I hate explaining myself or forcing my ears to be deaf.
I hate my eating disorder and my obsession to put things in order.
I hate narrow-minded people and my lips when they turn purple.
I hate my sweaty hands and accepting stupid commands.
I hate overthinking and sometimes the rushed decision making.
I hate a toxic environment and an unnecessary involvement.
I hate unproductive reading and regretting doing something.
I hate losing folks that I trusted and being in a situation that's twisted.
I hate a bad culture and acting after a disaster.
I hate irresponsibility and talking with irrationality.
I hate unfaithfulness and being so powerless.
I hate being unheard and encountering a complete nerd.
I hate unresolved matters and abusive monsters.
I hate wasting time and unwillingly paying even a dime.
I hate mystery and spreading a wrong story.
I hate being controlled and only doing as I am told.

I hate that I hate all of the above, it makes it even hard to be person to love.

28.02.2020

Hopeless Creature

A Saturday evening, I'm sitting on a chair.
Overthinking my life, I want to speed up the future.
Learning things that I won't probably apply,
Shush! Don't even ask me the how and the what and the why.
I'm already possessed by my stupid thoughts,
ok... some may be creative, but others are definitely not.
Oh, I know, days will obviously go by.
I want to understand this, trust me I try.
My body and brain are going neck to neck,
while courage, strength and patience are stuff I'm aiming to
collect.
But, if living is tied to torture,
what can I do as a hopeless creature?

19.12.2019

Documentary

That documentary got me so mesmerized,
despite how horrible it is being victimized.
I'm hoping to be part of that crowd,
I want to share my talent with the globe.
My trademark is held hostage in this office,
It's not how I imagine myself in a couple of years.
We were told not to dream and follow a safe road,
maybe I should deny my fear and "pursue" what I love the most.
I don't need to be LinkedIn and kill my spirit with an unnecessary
skill.
All I have to do is perfect my gift and go for the thrill.
I don't want another CV to fill.
I'm a woman full of a million will.
I want to be stuck in the studio and create some sounds for the
world to listen.
I want to spend sleepless nights inventing and enjoying my only
passion.
Time is flying by and I'm here writing about the spineless person
that I am.
Sometimes I even cry to remind me that it is pointless to blame.
I was offered the chance to see God's signs,
by being in a workplace I'm turning some blind eyes.
I'll be easily forgotten and replaceable.
So, I should let it go and show them of what I'm really capable.

10.02.2020

Thoughts

It's been 4 years since I've changed. Deep inside, I'm still the same.
Tough as a rock, that's who I used to be in the witness of the folks
who've been around for so long.
They know better of me; they saw what strangers couldn't see.
It saddens me even harder that I'm wrecked, for no valid reasons.
A big chaos is haunting my brain, and as days go a little darker,
a mess goes in my head, I'm such an overthinker.
Wish that I can let go of all this; to be honest there is nothing that
big to miss.
My energy's already consumed,
Yeah, I know, I'm already doomed.

03.04.2019

Blossom with your BAEs

To all the men that happened to take part of my journey...
I would like to tell you; you should be blessed that I pushed you
away.
That I made you take the decision to leave and never stay.
When I see you blossom with your BAEs,
and most of you are now married,
I thank GOD for being a negligent reason behind your happiness.
This is not a rosy speech, I have to say it,
Rather a thought that crossed my mind, so I wanted to embed it.
Even if I feel a little weird hearing that you're getting wedded,
I'm still flattered that at least one of you got me invited.
Maybe some of the stories didn't end well, and I'm the type that
moves on: I never dwell.
but most of you tales were wrapped beautifully regardless of being
out of touch today.
Time had to do its part and only time is the one to blame.
But fate to me is not that one eternal thing.
Fate is in all the small pieces that make anything into something.

07.06.2022

Toast

See me socialize,
but let me emphasize,
on what I despise the most.
Freaks in disguise, do bad and don't apologize.
Notice the size of their toast!
Don't be shocked,
things have sucked.
Tired of explaining,
tired of complaining.
Don't care about their impressions.
They'll highlight my imperfections,
so, I'll give them satisfaction and accept their rejections.
No more paranoia, and let me do that for you,
I'm a witch, so don't tag along.
It's always that way, my gut is never wrong.

27.02.2020

Thread instead

Sitting on a thread,
why I am afraid.
thinking about the mess in my head,
wanting to go to bed,
and I'm awake instead.
My eyes are wide open,
this is happening too often,
I'm solving the riddle,
putting the pieces of the puzzle.
It's actually a hard level.
Feels like my journey's cursed by a devil.
Counting down the hours and the minutes.
Hoping that this time, it actually fits.
New chances are all I wish.
I don't need to eat it, teach me how to fish.

17.02.2020

Back

I found it, I got myself back,
I know it, I got off track.
It helped by being standoffish and maybe a little bit selfish.
It's not arguable, I was so miserable.
It's indisputable, I was unapproachable.
Oh my god, that was so literal.
I mean, it had to be cynical.
Cheers to the old me,
so happy that I could foresee things that I had to flee.
Moods that I had to fix.
Guess that I missed out on being twenty-six.

11.01.2020

If we ever met again

If we ever met again, let us speak about the things that we left unsaid.
If we ever met again, let us do all the things that we didn't back then.
If we ever met again, don't tell me anything about the reason you fled.
If we ever met again, move right back to the time I was your special someone.
If we ever met again, leave a room to get to know me so that you can own me.
If we ever met again, you should think all this through, how precious am I to you.
If we ever met again, we don't want this to shuffle, and relive the same struggle.
If we ever met again, if we ever met again.

30.08.2020

Again, and again

Laying under a pile of stress,
it's been a while in this emotional distress.
It's always the same orbit,
too young to be resting for just a bit.
Too soon to be this fed up,
too little to say it's messed up.
Others might've seen worse, that's for sure!
I'm angry for taking everything to the core.
I'm frightened by my sickening nightmares,
and my heart is in a race, but who cares?
Aiming for an aim to be set,
hoping that my heart will finally speak for itself.
The ending is still very blurry, despite the struggle and the worries.
So, I go for temporary shelters.
A lot of ice cream, some loud music ... no filters,
not caring for what my annoying neighbors might say,
not thinking about the numbers on that scale, until the day it will
all blow up again, and I go back to where it all began.

08.07.2020

Forgotten

I was cruel enough to wipe you out of my memories.
I laughed off the way you spoke about our stories,
the ones I forgot that they existed, but I didn't forget that you
loved me more than I've ever expected.
You carried with you all of my pain, and you felt it again and
again.
Half a decade has passed, and your feelings did not fade, and you
never missed a year without wishing me a happy birthday. Yet I
ghosted your sweet wishes, and again I was one of those bitches.
You kept professing your feelings, and you never gave a damn
about all the yikes. You did whatever it takes, to embrace my flaws.
26.07.2020

Passive rejection

I often underline how badly I cannot trust folks.
A completely normal thing when all I do is focusing on jerks.
Whenever I think of making the slightest exception, bam! I get
slapped right in the face with a very passive rejection,
yet this time, it's different,
not the rejection though, that's just so frequent,
but the way I started dealing with the trauma,
and how everything took its natural place, I let it all to karma.
and oh mama! how that felt incredible,
though it still seems unbelievable,
but I broke that cursed cycle,
of the self-blame and hatred,
of the fake it 'till you make it,
once I had that one conversation with my
friend, I realized more that men's vision is so far from women's.
That we take the simplest moments and cherish them forever,
while they end it and move on like it didn't even happen.

03.02.2022

Lebanon

I have only been there once but something about you hits a very
soft spot in my heart.
It was long ago, way before we built a family and some friends
there.
A strong connection drew me to you right from the start,
maybe because speaking your dialect brings out a new shade of me,
or maybe because of an inner power that we cannot foresee.
Lebanon, you have already suffered enough pain that's why I'm
quite sure that your screams will not go in vain.
Despite the wars and terrorism, your people never lacked any
humanism.
The corruption and the economic downfall wrapped up the
misery that you have seen it all.
We can't miss that turning point further to that assassination, but
you survived all of it and for that you deserve a standing ovation.
Beirut was your golden rose,
in a split of a second, everything exploded.
One day, your sorrows will go away,
One day, no one will ever leave you, in peace they'll live, they'll
stay.

09.08.2020

Seasons

I have this urge to blame it all on the seasons,
I'd rather do it than exhibit my reasons.
I Don't really know if it's an all-night nightmare or a dream, or if
it's my self-consciousness or an end of a tunnel's beam.
Rolling under this coaster of emotions,
flashbacking my life in slow motions,
attempting to explain these notions,
healing through endless devotions,
not giving a jack about promotions or demotions.
In the end, what matters isn't your status,
and in life, you are just a tiny fetus.
When I hear these speeches, I can't stop rolling my eyes.
When these words are coming from demons in disguise, who
conspire against the innocent,
"fake it 'till you make it" to be pleasant,
talking behind the walls to shelter from the wows, pushing you to
your limits and shutting you up when you speak out.
No one can deprive me from my right,
if you cross the line, you're so out.

01.10.2020

***ck

I'm learning to hold it all back.
Not to let my emotions crack.
To keep them steady, keep them stacked.
I'm not claiming to be an expert in this area and I'm still not a
quack.
But I mastered certain aspects in life and for that I have a knack.
It was neither a bright white nor a pitch black,
yet I can write a book about my whole pack,
it can narrate to you when I got up and when I received a whack,
and how I've always believed that I lacked some luck.

25.09.2020

Intact

She frustrates me to the core that I have nothing left to offer but hatred. Even when I want to be warm, the bruises fill me up and I feel like an idiot.
The darkest spots never took a toll on me, but the tiniest things she does is what I loathe to see.
How can I be part of her life and not share a single value?
Not the physical ones but the morals that I thought I maintained and knew, writing this certainly looks like a sin and it just sounds obnoxious, but this anarchy should've been different and I shouldn't feel anxious.
I gained a lot of strength while growing up since no one could lead that household,
whereas that wasn't my role if truth is being told.
The life threatening decisions that I took at the age of twelve, all of the scary missions that she encountered should've made her dwell, as if she reached any simple goals... she never did well.
Even when death was threatening her little girls, she still ran after hell.
If I compare her to all the other species, she's on the spectrum of JUST BAD.
If we retract the history, it will forever stay intact.
Every time I grab my phone to write something cool,
I become immersed in the hate and I sound like a fool.
It's like I'm a prisoner of these loops but I still want to stick to my roots.

25.11.2020

Last bit of pride

When I heard about that one last piece of information that I
ignored all four years since it ever happened,
everything changed in me, It felt like, literally, my entire world had
collapsed.
I knew that my destiny was already rough but I was hanging on
that one bit of pride.
I've always been very open about it because I have absolutely
nothing to hide,
but that one thing made me feel betrayed.
It sucks when the whole world is aware of it and you, the
concerned one, don't.
The words defeated me and it was like I was living in an ultimate
lie.
Yeah, it's not a big deal when your life isn't on the line, or it's not
like I was going to die.
But I have to learn the mains and the sides,
and all of the details about my life.
So it was a shattering truth,
that I was a victim of a scheme or a spoof.
I wanted to snooze the alarm,
to protect my heart from any harm,
and in order to save again my pride,
I had to let another thing slide.

16.09.2020

My genes

You know that my genes do not belong to their type of mold.
Despite the imaginary scenes, my truth is always told.
The chemicals composing me cannot adjust to that kind of
culture.
Be part of that circus and you'll see yourself the full picture.
You'll know their dusty colors and their passive torture.
They press all of your buttons and expect the grenade to be off,
I've reached the highest mountains and enough is enough.
If this is a patience test, I'll be happy to fail.
I'll welcome you as my guest but you'll never get a part in my tale.

08.10.2020

Pandemic

We called it a pandemic to give a sense that the world is always
united.
In reality, everyone is dealing with their own epidemic which
means we're already shattered.
Prioritizing the paramedics, these folks are saving people's lives.
According to statistics, front lining is like holding shives.
Now that the risk is approaching and getting to your entourage,
it's unwillingly reminding you that it's an absolute sabotage:
"Wash your hands and wear your masks!".
Though these sound like some freaking easy tasks,
it's suffocating man! not just in the air we don't get to breathe, but
also in every single thing that serves as a sheathe.
We asked the question billions of times already,
since the situation doesn't look like it's monitored, it's never
steady.
But where's this thing going?
what the hell are we even doing?

09.10.2020

Bubbly

You didn't seem like a bubbly person,
but you were the only one there who's part of my generation.
I learnt who "Millennials" are through you,
and the word "baby boomers" too.
I've never understood what was attractive about you,
but now that I can name it, it's my love language that you knew.
You unchecked all of the items on my list,
you made me forget it and follow my guts.
The soft spoken words that changed the knobs of my heart,
the long vulnerable conversations that bewitched me from the
start.
Your kid-like smiles and cute giggles,
your super kind eyes and the romantic candles.
The random selfies on WhatsApp,
and the video calls on every single app.
You gave me a full package and then let go,
you made me question if I was the one at fault,
but you're the one who broke the promises.
You completely vanished and left me with the unlived premises.
I'm not sure if I'm grieving your loss, or if it's my past that I want
to toss, or it's these lyrics that came across,
to change the current era that is full of flaws.
Thus, consider this another stop, another pause,
and it's up to you to relate to this or simply pass.

10.01.2021

Hearts are not for fun.

You showed up in my life unwelcomed, and it's my home you trespassed.
You built a bubble of dreams being all sure that "we will last".
So, I let you in, but you escaped from it so fast.
Now I see that you're the only one who had a blast!
You claimed to love me while you know how hard it is for me to believe anyone.
If you wanted a toy, you should've bought one...
You should know better... You should know that hearts are not for fun.
and that in my land, that's not how things are done.
If I protected myself for three decades and you still sneaked in, it means that I only saw you from a deeper end.
I disregarded the details that would normally make me run away, and my insecurities? they were vanishing, day after day.
I started getting dolled up... my routine included glam.
Although I didn't like to, I introduced you to my fam.
I left all idols and stars to follow... I became your number one fan.
I never expected that to be part of your plan.
I never expected you to be my first love, to be my man.
I'm still shocked at the boundaries I crossed.
Would I recover the old me, the one I lost?
You wanted to boast to the world that I'd be your fiancée.
And just like that, you were my Jay-Z and I was your Beyoncé, but even Queen B got cheated on.
Guess it's part of growing up. Guess that I'll just have to move on.

08.09.2022

Era

If I monitor my temper,
I simply feel out of character.
If I keep it all in,
the inner exploding will end up happening.
My feelings are not just about anger,
bottling it up grows it bigger and bigger.
I want to end that bad era,
I want to improve and be better.

07.12.2020

Third decade

No wonder how people rarely get through their sixth milestone.
I'm barely in my third decade and I'm already wondering how I can carry on.
Things turn easily boring no matter how hard I try to be innovative.
I'm not saying that I'm ungrateful, proof is how I always want to be creative.
I thought that I'd give it a try at YouTube even though I knew that it wasn't for me.
One year later, most of my subscribers are just friends and family.
I thought that I'd give it a try at losing weight, something that I've been trained to do but I went back to binge eating and gaining more than what I originally had.
I thought that I'd give it a try at dating, but I ended up being part of an unscripted play that you'd still applause even if it's ridiculously fake.
I thought that I'd give it a try at socializing by going all out and extending my network, but I got reminded that if I don't make the plans, nobody includes me in theirs.
I thought that I'd give it a try at being successful at my job, so I worked my ass off like always, but I figured that they made me climb a ladder I never wanted, doing even more boring stuff than what I pictured.
I thought that I'd give it a try at writing, after all that's what I do daily, but here I am on my third attempt, and I don't even know if I'm going to finish anything.

It's like I reach the middle of the road and then get back to the starting point. That's exactly what drives me crazy most of the time : the fact that I realize that it could've taken the same energy to reach the finish line, but I quit and left it all behind.
It might be my impatience or that I was programmed to function at a maximum speed.
It might be the life equation: sometimes you heal and sometimes you bleed.
When I enter that singing lesson, I feel for a while how it's seriously therapeutic.
Right when the teacher says something that hits me in deep, it confuses me to the point I question if it's because of her words or because of my genetics.
Am I just emotional or are my feelings just erratic?
Am I digging a hole in my brain or am I being dramatic?
Great thing that I talk to myself every day.
Great thing that I can put labels to my state.
But truth is what I want to say today : I don't know if I'll ever find my way or if my approach in life will make me sustain.

15.11.2022

You fooled me.

I'm not the type to follow any sign but when it comes to you, I wanted to believe that you were mine.
If the world put us together in the same space, I hoped that I could be the one to replace...
All your sorrows and hardships...
Be your tomorrows and fellowships...
I never knew that height mattered to me until I fell for your 6.2 feet.
I never knew that blue eyes bewitch me until I caught myself looking at yours on repeat.
I never knew I was cringy until I said that you made me complete, and I never knew that you fooled me until I learnt how to be deceived.
All the above was not your fault, you did not make your physique after all.
I mean... I was attracted to... all the things that were not the real you:
Your remarks about my outfits and highlights on if I wore make-up or not.
"He must be so interested in me" that's what I thought.
Hating on kids and changing your mind when I said I liked them.
Saving me a spot at our morning coffee shop, that's what you did back then.
Buying me food and eating the desserts that you said you disliked, joining meetings while sharing the same earphones... What a sight!

Making the whole office create rumors about us, and when
confronted about your feelings... You acted in disgust.
My bad for believing that we were getting close... My bad for
getting ideas that were wrong.
Were they really wrong? Was I delusional as my friend said?
Did I exaggerate what we had?
Am I really a rookie in love? Did that make you laugh?
I wish I had a superpower that reads your mind,
I wish I could find what I had to find,
before finally understanding that you fooled me.
I wish I had lenses that captured what we had so that I can show
them to my bestie.
She would at least speak based on facts and not assumptions.
I would know what was real and what wasn't based on her
reactions.
Now I have to say this before it's too late,
I might haven't forgotten about you yet,
but I will for my sake... let this be our bet.

10.04.2022

Don't you dare.

Don't you dare say even once that I "abandoned you" when I spent 7 years of my life waiting for you to "fix yourself".
I, who kept on convincing my mind that you deserved a second chance, until you got used to it and I turned into dust on unread books or empty shelves.
I ignored every single cue; I dismissed every single red flag too.
Deep down, my gut pinched me, and it was urging me to stop watching your infinite play, but what could my heart say when it was all swayed?
I was playing it the unromantic and the insensitive type when my soul was drying up pushing me to think that it's normal to sacrifice that much for love,
it's normal to question my actions and my values when I've always known that things are not normal like that.
Every time we break up, it was another step to making things stop by putting an end to manipulation and lies,
to gaslighting and denials,
to slacking off and forgetting that we had lives,
and I'm no longer accepting to let my precious years pass by.
I don't want you to think that I'm doing this because I'm 29 and that my ship has "sailed".
I want you to know that a brand new luxurious one has arrived in my shore,
and I'm breaking free from the old naive me, I'm letting the new warrior sink into the core.
I'm not regretting you whatsoever, although I did hope for things to be better.

Instead of the fights and the arguments, I wanted for us to love
deeply and build a healthy future together.
But I guess that I wasn't meant to be your
wife and you weren't meant to be my husband but just another
lesson in life.

04.04.2023

Hey Doctor!

Hey Doctor! I'm here to get a proper diagnosis.
I need to before any sentimental paralysis.
Where do I start with these many introductions?
I no longer can identify where things went terribly wrong, how it
went from pop to a very sad song.
My life looks snoozed from afar,
but deep down I'm as damaged as a crashed car.
I'm constantly attracting trouble,
and I'm not even a soldier in an uphill battle.
I've done every online test since the symptoms filled up the space,
and I found millions of answers to bring back my grace.
But I need a specialist's take on this,
So please tell me what the hell is my case?
Tell me if what I do is in the name of healing,
or if I've been fooling myself and just kept on lying.
If I really don't care about dying,
or if all these people will be all happy about it and smiling. If my
name will be just a memory,
or a link to a very shameful story,
of a girl who was brighter than a sunlight,
giggles and laughter never left her life,
and then she switched to a nasty version.
Now she's got lingering feelings to recover the original.
Doctor, do you really have the answers to my questions, or shall I
just leave and deal with the tensions?

22.12.2020

Tornado

Speaking to you even though my words were kind of messy.
You got to know that nothing of what you're reflecting on is crazy.
It's something that you have to go through to grow and improve.
So, don't be cruel to your soul.
Your consciousness is there to get you out of your sad groove,
and I said this already but I want you to embrace your flaws and
keep on going.
Pick up any small chances and ignore everything that is annoying.
Albeit the wind may look like a tornado, you have to cope with it
and survive.
You can gain the mental fight if you go with everything you have.
Just don't give in and you'll end up winning.

24.11.2020

Our region

I thought that you were a foreigner at first since your profile said
you were living abroad.
So, I spoke in English with you while you answered me in our
dialect, and I felt like a fool, man!
Although your last name hinted to our region, I excluded that
theory because you might be from the middle east, or maybe, you
were born there or you're an external consultant... to say the least.
We were these normal people that frequently talked about work
right from the start, but who would've imagined that we shared
the same crazy thing we call art.
That's why I'm so grateful that you decided to gift me your
amazing book, seven whole months with no clue... I can't believe
how long it took,
but I read the whole thing in three days, and I'm glad to learn that
I'm among the few who understood your cryptic ways.
That I could read between the lines, caught on the signals of your
old and recent times.
That I was able to discuss it directly with the author and see things
through the lenses of the creator.
It's forever a delight that people open up to me,
that I as well summarize the pages of my ongoing story.
To exchange the deep emotions and visions,
and forget about the "what happened" and the silly reasons.
I said that everyone is a temporary stop in our lives,
but like every beginning, I wish that the connection I share with
people survives.

26.01.2022

Betimes

I grabbed my phone and searched for the Notes' App. It's what I
do when I rewind the relapse. I doodle my thoughts and make
them sync to these verses forcing harmony,
but if I'm being honest, reality is a melodramatic sort of felony.
Though it sounds peaceful and I might even be someone's idol, I'm
not sure if I'm in a position to be a role model. What you see is just
a displayed shell. What's within, is a story I can't really tell.
Actually, these glimpses are all in my head, I can't interpret my
fate, but I'll fix the imagination I fed. I'd work on positivizing my
lines, I'll be revising them for the betimes.

20.11.2020

Tradeoff

It took me so long, to know what went wrong.
All the things that I have learnt all along without you,
and now that you're gone, I started to mourn.
If I knew that losing you is a tradeoff,
to find another kind of love,
the sort that I've always craved,
then what I had was more than enough.
The purest with no barriers or conditions,
the craziest with all it sacrifices and blessings.

07.11.2020

Attached

It's silly but these temporary bits of memories keep me going.
It's like nurturing this empty soul of mine from time to time.
I never cease to go for it, maintain the vibe, make it flow.
Albeit our EGOs where stronger than what we had,
it's still a feeling that made me glad,
to be sincere, nothing was special, and I was just trying to be
social.
Two months of boredom were filled by your presence,
most of which was nothing but complete nonsense.
We were just keeping each other's companies,
and trying to get rid of the simple everyday stories.
You started to get attached and you knew that I was out of your
league,
and I started to get detached and blame it all on the fatigue.
I allowed you to take the lead,
but never did I ever show you my entire feed.
That was my free self-gifted deed,
because I realize that things will tend to be weird.
That you'll just be another song feat.
Facts prove me right once more,
you're just another one I had to annoy.

22.06.2021

Best Couple

I strongly believe in destiny if they were the only couple I see.
They said the dorm's gym was their starting point,
but how could that happen if she was there for barely a month?
Two widely separate worlds came united through an infinite
chemistry. Completely different in aspects but they see eye to eye
when it comes to family.
When our cousin said she wanted someone to lift her up all the
way, I was like, girl! that's what they did to each other every day.
That's what fortified the entanglement regardless of the occasional
fights.
They know how to show affection and how to get over with the
long and boring nights.
Now I'm seeing them as parents, I don't know about other people,
but they've definitely got the mold of parenthood. Bless that little
cutie soul they just had, and guys, let's knock on some wood.
They got people from across the world to gather,
they made of me an auntie, so thank you for our beautiful Nana,
Your big warm hearts will get you through it all.

18.07.2021

CMS

I know that I haven't seen you ever since the pandemic hit the
world,
and I know that I should've sent you my farewell all along.
I know that we got caught by life and its twists,
especially when life didn't do you any justice...
I actually hate the thought that my memories of you are blurred
now,
and I hate to admit that I have forgotten about you... somehow...
I'm not sure if it's denial or if it's the fact that my brain stopped
processing shocking news.
It's fucking me up because you don't deserve any of the shit that's
happening to you.
When you said that I was like a daughter to you, you proved that
just right.
When that bitch was crossing her
boundaries, you stood for me like a soldier leading a fight. You
gave me an opportunity of a lifetime, and you paved the way for at
least half a decade to come...
I learnt a lot from you professionally for sure.
I wouldn't be doing what I'm doing today if it wasn't partially
thanks to you.
Your generosity was beyond imagination...
Your strong character will forever be my aspiration.
You were a very giving man, to everyone including strangers.
And your wise words are still with me until this day, I still quote
them as if I heard them yesterday.

" There's always a red line. Don't let whoever bastard cross it and just put them back to their places", and even if I wasn't feeling like it that year, I stand by that value in spite of my wavering phases.
The last image of you is of a very charismatic chief.
That image will always shine in my brain...that's my belief...
It was supposed to be your time of relief. It was supposed to be your well-deserved retirement.
Yet an hour ago, they told me that it's a matter of a 72-hour. It means that the poison had you all devoured.
I wish that you could celebrate the victory like I did 7 years ago.... I wish that I'm not sitting here writing about how fast you have to go.
Other than prayers and some few words to honor you, it's sickening that it's all I'm capable to do...

28.04.2022

Colors

Would you tell me we're the same if you saw my colors change?
I would notice the cloudy days, but I still find my own ways, to
wrap my head around that state and fill in excuses until this date.
Shining stars and burning summer heats,
crowded bars and hearts skipping beats,
lengthy chats and few hours of sleep,
silly's on and smart went on bleep.
You dragged this all along and you pretend that nothing's wrong,
and I experience the same cycle again and I have nothing left to
prolong.

20.05.2021

Get it freed.

This is to all of you, the scaredy cats I keep on facing.
Those who throw me in hell to celebrate their winnings,
with whom I saw endings before beginnings,
the ones who would love to highlight my weakest points.
Little do they know that they're my strongest traits,
I grow from the despair of despising the old F,
now that I'm finally loving myself,
forcing me to change isn't happening,
since I'm convinced that it's the right path that I'm following.
You can tell how proud I am of the new me,
It's pretty clear, it's easy to see,
and now that I won't want my lyrics to bleed, I had to let it
breathe, let it freed.

18.02.2021

I see you.

I see you... Take away all the beautiful lives.
Deprive us all from their presence, their smiles.
I see you... In every corner of my memory and in every scar on my
body.
In every "Thank you" and in every "Sorry".
I see you... Through my mood swings and
through all the unexplainable things.
Maybe through the thick and thin.
I see you... Creating a hole in every family and being a very
terrifying enemy, and your existence... it should be regarded as a
felony!
I see you... Between the fears of a checkup and underneath any
serious hiccup.
In all the heavy bills and even via a flu syrup.
I see you... Filling up jars of tears and sweats of sturdy hills. Picking
up prayers such as "We wish it heals".
Wondering how it actually feels to be your victim.
When you're something nobody seems to fathom.
Even the healthiest ones among us lost against you.
Even the youngest ones didn't find strength to fight you.
That's why I still see you... In the eyes of my cousin who was barely
thirty.
Or my uncle who couldn't celebrate being fifty.
I see you... In my boss who recently retired and couldn't get to
enjoy his precious time.
In the other beloved ones that are now gone.
I see you... everywhere I go.

You're not hiding, you just carry on. I see you while it's hard not
fall.
I see you... breaking my highest wall.
I see you and I don't want to see you anymore.

24.05.2022

Instead of mourning

I was taught to believe in heaven, so I thought that you were my
guardian angel.
That my cupid of love said enough is enough, "I got you a partner
for life!"...
He created the silliest reasons for us to be together and I saw us
being happy forever.
I knew that we came from different backgrounds and that there
was no way for us to be that close,
but as cocky as it sounds, you're the only person I chose.
Coming out of a messy break-up, you wanted me to heal.
None of the things you told me were made-up, everything was
real.
You confessed to me that it's a first for you to be that bold and tell
someone not to fall for you,
and despite everyone's warnings, including my best mates, I kept
on insisting that I do.
I don't know if it's because of the twisted events that got me
addicted, got me attached.
Or it's because of all we've been through that you had my heart
snatched.
I admit that you were honest about us and about your feelings.
I was your best friend... someone you talked to so easily.
Someone you call at 2am in the morning... Someone with whom
you roam around the city instead of mourning.
Someone you showed your cheerful self to when things were
falling apart.

and that letter you wrote me, I still have it with me and think that
it's a pure art.
The words you mentioned strengthened me in my weakest era,
But I hoped to have you physically next to me instead of that piece
of paper.
I was the first to celebrate your birthday as an adult, but when it
all came down you blamed it on me: " It's solely your fault!".
How can you encourage me to embrace my emotions and then ask
me to suppress my love for you?
How can you talk to me 24/7 and then you suddenly withdrew?
You gave me no explanation to why you pushed me away,
and the farther you pushed, the harder I
committed to stay.
You left no room for contact; you left no room for us to talk.
I held onto the chance to hear from you via your friends' social
media, I never intended to creep you.
Why did you leave me hanging for 4 years waiting for you to come
back? Did I deserve that harsh treatment when all I did was to
have your back?
I was literally there for you in the thick and thin.
I never judged you and only saw you from deep within.
When you finally messaged me in October, my gut told me that it
was finally over.
Not us, but the farewell your forced on me.
I wished that you were a little gentle after all these years... I wished
that you dissed me while wiping your tears.
You came to tell me that you're no longer the same person,
but my heart couldn't see you any different.
I don't know if I should be grateful for how we untangled.
I don't know if it's thanks to you that I immigrated.

I don't know why things didn't go as I wished they would.
But I do know that I did the best I could.
Continuing to love you... I don't know if I should.
Even though I wanted you to be the ONE, I think that I can now
be with anyone.

17.04.2022

MNJ – The start

Complete randomness popped you up in front of me.
I don't care about anything else, not even romantically.
All I do care about is keeping you right beside me, in any shape or form that is.
Your cheerful side is what I missed,
and so is your vulnerability,
and your high sense of responsibility.
You talk about it all, but you also hide your bruises,
and I tend to never get sick of hearing these painful doses.
A person with a lot of baggage that I want to embrace.
A kid at heart, and a cute smiling face.
Reminding me that healing is one hell of a process,
that emotions can get stuck at times, something we need to confess.
It's quite rare for someone to touch my soul deeply.
I might require endless energy and effort, but somehow, I'm letting go of that thought easily.
Humbled again about life and its unexpected spins,
not paying attention to whether it's about losses or wins.
As we never know how the future will turn out to be,
I hope that I at least bring in my expertise and let you open up more to me.
I may contribute to mending one part of you.
If I ever do, that would be a great accomplishment and a happy move.

24.12.2021

MNJ – The end

A shoutout to what I wrote last week,
oh god, I can't believe that I said what I said,
and how things turned out to be super weird.
When I read the lines and the delivered emotions,
and I'm sitting here laughing about my lack of devotion,
and how I'm stuck in the same damned cycle,
of the push and pull, the ghosting toll,
every amazing sign and then the forever fucked-up bull.
Well you know what? I'm sick of being the bad bitch when I'm
actually not.
I'm tired of going through the same bipolar zodiacs.
When I behave well and try to feel secure and commit, it's like
binge eating while I want to be fit.
Then I receive a trigger to my trust issues,
which makes me question every single person I knew,
and think that maybe I'm the one at fault.
Well, every time that shit happens, I know that I'm not.
If it was the case I'd deal with it on the spot,
I don't run from my wrongdoings, and I admit it when I fuck up.
If they think that only them have that bit of a pride,
I want to still remind them that I also love that ride,
of how I redeem and preserve my ego and my dignity,
and that's how I tell you, babe, you lost me until the infinity.

14.01.2022

K.

Ever since our first encounter, I was a girl he had to flag,
which got me confused because we just played laser tag.
Then we met again through a group of friends,
the atmosphere was pretty cold and dense.
I remember playing cards with him while everyone else was
uninterested.
It's right when our chemistry got manifested,
and I didn't need to test it,
I instantly knew it. He fell for my unusual spell.
It was so easy to tell.
It's love that I smelled,
and devotion that I spelled.
He was the shy type, so he didn't want to make it obvious,
but he liked that I was an open book and
that I wasn't mysterious.
He happened to come during an emotional wreck.
I gave away a strong aura which made him be taken aback.
He enjoyed my chatty nature and my cheerful vibes,
little did he know that I easily switch sides.
That he saw my heights and did not expect the lows.
He just followed his guts and the dopey flows.
He blindly loved an imaginary version.
He badly loved a bipolar person.
He suffered more yet he persisted to check on me.
I know that I'm the ultimate one to blame here, but I couldn't love
him the way he did.
Love comes with the heart and not with the fist.

He had to reckon that it was just a close friendship, and that it was an emotional intimacy that he sipped.

19.01.2021

Normal

When she was young, she wanted to have a normal life like all the folks she bumped into, but normal isn't for everyone... normal isn't necessarily "normal" too.

She thought of a billion occupations that she could handle. In fact, she did her best to nail everything in this jungle.

She postponed "the big plans" as she grew into her twenties until she realized it wasn't her call.

Luckily, she found the one that kept her company despite it all.

He made sure to support her in every move and be there for her even when things got a little crazy.

She didn't understand him at first: she thought that his demeanor was a bit hazy. Then, as time flew by, he proved her wrong...that she can finally trust a man.

So, she let go of her fears and she enjoyed their incredible adventures as if he was the idol and she was his fan.

After three years together, they decided to get married and go to Thailand for their honeymoon.

The wedding ceremony went amazing, there wasn't a social earthquake but there was an emotional typhoon.

Actually, happiness invaded the air. However, happiness isn't always fair.

She felt it in her bones. She felt like she was living a very unimaginable dream.

That's when life gave her an unrecoverable strike and that's when she lost her beam.

Her husband of only 14 days had passed after going for his last surf. He vanished in that big ocean, and she had to take the shocking reality.
The trauma of him leaving the turf... the feeling of despair and fatality.
The little girl crossed the dark tunnel... going from the wife to the widow...
Albeit, the title didn't matter, his absence did.
How can she carry on without him? Why is their thread so thin?
Can she overcome what people say? the jerks who ridicule her pain?
Time. Time healed her mental disorder but will never heal the outrageous feeling of that experience.
That's what she thought when she realized that even from above, he guided her to her vocation.
She's now helping people who are as wrecked as she used to be.
She's going down the road of counselling.
Sharing her story, giving away a lot of empathy.
That's what she had to spread instead of solely focusing on sympathy.
The moral of this is that life brings you a lot of dualities.
If you're too sad: that will teach you how to be glad.
and if you're too content, it will project to you what sorrow meant.

01.04.2022

Brighter

When she came in, she made his dark world way brighter.
She embraced his insecurities and pushed him to be stronger.
She highlighted his best traits and taught him to appreciate
everything he considered a clutter.
What he saw as a mess, she found details that she considered a
progress.
When his self-confidence was on the low, she approached him
with a rhythm that is slow.
Never did she leave, never did she go.
When life gave him a blow, she was sure that he'd know,
that no matter what happened, she'd be his buddy.
She'd be the person who deserved to be the one who he confided
in,
who deserved to be part of a trip he never chose to dive in.
Things never made sense before, he even built-up higher walls,
when he was a dreamer and got deceived,
now things got realer, and he got them misperceived.
But at least he tried for her. He tried to follow her road.
She made him laugh and spread a cheerful energy around
everyone.
But when her positive container wasn't filled back, her other side
got switched on.
She got to a dead end : two negatives might turn to positives in
math, but things don't work like that in real life.
If two clouds gather, they turn into rain. And if the rain doesn't
stop, the floods would fill up drains.
And everybody knows what comes next.

Expect the worst and never the best and if you want to add a little touch of despair, and stress that pile up... things never turn out to be fair.
Because when she needed support, he had nothing to give her.
When she wanted to be understood, he behaved like a complete stranger.
He expressed contradicting opinions. He hurt her feelings. What's even worse is that he never confessed or apologized for it. He didn't attempt to fix things or address his wrongdoings and just like that, he let her go.
and just like that she had another fact, that either you open your book, or you close it,
things will forever end the same way.

09.01.2023

My situation

Albeit I was saying that it was fine, it was normal, after all it was
fated to be so.
I never truly believed it when it came from other people's
perspective,
it's like pretending to feel the pain when you weren't the one being
in it.
I never blamed them either since they were supporting me
through this.
Though some were honest and made it clear that they would never
accept this situation.
Others stayed quiet and pretended that they didn't hear it.
Then there is this one who stood out among the crowd.
Who told me it was silly to bail on me and that I should be proud.
That I was a real fighter and should not be tough on myself.
That sometimes all you need is a little help,
I know that this stranger was there for a reason.
Well, he came back after a certain while for a second run,
despite being nasty with him, he returned and took me for who I
am.
The same night I heard that my personality stunk, and to be
honest I felt a little hurt when these words validated what I usually
think.
That I'm probably this very horrible person that everyone runs
away from,
that maybe all my extreme decisions were derived from what I
believed I was.

That I accepted me, but people didn't, and they've had enough of
my creepy dose.
Then, I got a new reminder that I'm not that bad,
that even my sister said that just because she was mad.
Let's face it, if you don't mess with me, I'm still an amazing buddy.
If you let me be, you'll know that I'm just as honest as everybody.

29.07.2021

Somebody that mattered.

It's funny how 5 days prior to this, I was saying that death no
longer bothered me.
Was it really death or simply the mention of any disease?
Well, I learnt that the hard way... what can I say?... Maybe I forgot
what it was like to lose somebody that mattered.
Or maybe the way he passed is what made my feelings all
scattered...
It's funny how I haven't seen him physically for over 2 years... yet,
when his soul left earth, that bad event brought back all the feels.
I know that I became an emotional wreck, but I still kept my
composure.
and I can't seem to disregard any detail that counts as pleasure:
Meeting him the first time...
being introduced to via my mom...
I remember him sitting on that long black chair...
He was sipping his coffee and making jokes with his subordinates.
I knew it then that he was a very cool boss.
I didn't see fear in people's eyes. I saw joy... looking at someone
they looked up to.
I don't deny being intimidated by his strong aura... his very
charming character too.
Public speaking was an easy process for him.
He actually nailed that even on a whim.
He introduced me to diverse subjects at work... man! how time
flies.
He even checked on me during the rough times...

Not to mention the infinite list of gifts: He really did consider me as a family member.
He was born to be a great leader and that's why he climbed that ladder.
Traveling the world and resolving conflicts.
In fact, his phone never left his hand as he replied to all the e-mails.
He truly loved his job albeit it was very hectic. If he sustained that environment for over 32 years, it can't be just a tactic.
It's funny how my brain stored all these pieces of information, and how we shared this strong connection...
I don't know about anything else, but this occurrence makes me a mess.
Maybe because I've tasted some of that venom... maybe because It's something I relate to...
Maybe because my defense mechanism blocked me from focusing on his last tiring journey.
Well, If I feel like this, I don't want to imagine what his relatives go through....
and I know that I said it's funny a lot... but it's funny how nothing of what I said is actually funny.

01.05.2022

The start of the end

After coming in terms with this whole story,
I still don't understand why I have to explain it every single time.
You asked me to retrieve its glory,
but now I feel trapped in the cycle of my life.
Sometimes I act like I'm elated non-purposely,
and I run after my endeavor crazily.
I read books to learn about vocations and my unresolved calling,
then my brain freezes in vacations, and I find myself falling.
I have pictured thousand jobs that I could nail,
but I was reluctant to do them, I was afraid I'd fail, and the perfect
family frame, I rejected that like I've rejected fame.
I built some solid walls around me, still earthquakes take few
seconds to get me.
I go back to constructions for years,
when I'm almost done with the mending,
I resume the state of fears.
I forge the happy mood with the help of food.
I stay alerted with the wrong dude,
I push him away and say we're good,
but they should understand that once my secret is out.
You'll see that I wasn't wrong, I was right.

29.04.2021

The transit

I met billions of people and I know when someone is just a transit.
Even if it feels surreal and life brought you suddenly together, it is what it is.
If they don't open up to you no matter how hard you try, they will forever remain as question marks.
It's not worth the analysis and the deciphering... mystery will always fill up your space.
and if you ask me how to digest that? I'll say that it just deepens your trust issues.
When you don't get the answers to simple questions, or don't get answers at all, your brain goes into the investigator mode and things will burn up there.
But why would anyone do that? it's already exploding as it is so why add up to that?
For whose sake? A regular passerby who would easily abandon you without looking back?
Everyone knows what they mean to people, but we sit there and wait while we crave for affection and attention.
Then we process departures and goodbyes differently and it hurts more when the habits are strong.
When you don't have that immediate replacement option and you have to make an effort for it to happen and go through that routine once again.
Major red flags are coming:
the " We talk on my own terms" jerk,
who loves to ask but hates to answer.
The "I like you, but I won't try to make it work",

who sweet talks you but thinks that you're too much to handle.
The " I fuck up but you're always wrong",
who will never budge in front of their ego.
The "I'm always right and people are weird"
who would just disappear and go.
The "We do understand differences",
but will disrespect the first one who's unsimilar to the way they
were raised.
The "I am who I am! Take me or leave me" shitty head,
who's never open to any positive change.
If you face one of those,
Just run my dear.
If you are one of those,
then make these bad traits disappear.
They will think that personal development is a delusional act,
don't worry, that's how silly people react.
So do your thing, improve and be better,
if you don't want to be the transit or don't want to attract the
latter.

20.06.2021

What could've been different.

Recently, I've been picturing what could've been different in the life I thought was boring.

If I didn't visit that doctor a decade ago, would the little monsters grow inside of me?

If I didn't play laser tag, would I have felt the "rocks" that already started building in?

If we didn't follow any recommendation, would I have gone to the same surgeon?

If he didn't misdiagnose me, would the benign tumor turn into cancer?

If any of the above didn't happen, would I still be infertile? Would I be this accepting?

If that surgery didn't occur, would life still find its way to make me feel miserable?

If I didn't reach out to the son of my father's acquaintance, would I have gone for IT and not management?

If I didn't love playing cards, would I ever be by the side of my current friends?

If I wasn't decisive, would I quit the field that I believed wasn't my fit?

If I wasn't free that year, would I have joined the United Nations?

If my people didn't continue to be students, would I sign in for the master's program while maintaining my occupation?

If my boss wasn't toxic, would I have been a witness to workplace harassment?

If I didn't talk to my homie about my career, would I have thought of pursuing O.M?

If our professor didn't bring that company over, would I have
known about it in between?
If their tasks didn't align with what I have been doing, would I
have joined their team?
If any of the above didn't happen, would I be thriving at my job?
Would I have solved my lifelong prob?
If I didn't get swayed by my classmate's words, would I have
created any armor?
If I have met any trustworthy person, would I have had any
long-term lover?
If I said no to my best friend at the time, would we still be going
strong? If I didn't block the one who loved me the most, would
the relationship feel wrong?
If I haven't had my share of people passing by, would I still be good
at goodbyes?
If any of the above didn't happen, would I notice that I'm not one
to be in a wedded bliss? Would I have known that I don't have any
chance to miss?

10.04.2022

Not even sorry

Separation used to hurt me before,
now it doesn't bother me anymore.
Not that I don't create deep holes emotionally, I really truly do.
But I don't allow them to cut me open by constantly reminding
myself that the past is the proof,
the proof that eternity is not human,
and that at the end of the story, we all become aloof.
It all comes back to my past and my spirit. It all comes back to
always choosing to exit.
I'll have to admit that I turn into an egocentric person, to the
point that relationships no longer matter to me.
I avoid everything that can likely harm me or cause the "bad
phase" to stay longer, and just like that, I only focus on saving me.
Basically, my type of separation is not physical or moral.
My type of separation is simply mental.
I split from reality, and I take my time to recharge.
Those who really know me would be patient and give me my
space.
And those who are busy dealing with their own issues and take my
mood personally, I don't want to put myself in their place.
When I'm down, I don't care about mending people's broken
pieces or letting go of the smallest annoying details.
I can barely get through this, and I don't mind if the rest of it fails.
So, to those who understood this without me having to explain it,
that's a big Thank you!
And to those who caught on the first downfall and fled... Well,
that's also a big Thank you!

You made it easier for me to not be the devil of the story!
And losing you never felt bad actually. I'm not even sorry!

26.09.2022

His world crumbled down.

He thought the world of her and that's when his entire world
crumbled down.
It's crazy what her love could do to him specifically when he
thought that she was the one.
She was someone who could get things done.
Bossy as ever and always upfront.
She resembled foxes with her attitude.
Maybe that's what got him lured.
She never seduced him though and it might be the reason why she
was very charming.
The aura was calming. But the character was daunting.
Her bubbly side hid it all, nothing was alarming.
And if you ask him what happened, he'd say that she was simply
enchanting.
You might get a little curious to know her secret,
or how things went wrong in the first place.
Here's the thing, she didn't have a dazzling beauty over which
you'd squint.
but damn, she got charisma... if that can be your hint!
Her intellect is beyond this world, notably on the emotional side
with the long talks she intuitively provides.
Although he's not that chatty, he'd tell you about her for hours.
With an excited and shaky voice, he'd narrate to you how it went
from sweet to sour.
How she no longer replied to his texts.
Something he never expected.
and he said he gets it, but he never understood her.

What's with her sudden change of heart?
Did he do something that bothered her?

04.07.2022

I wish.

I wish I could forget about you... like I thought I would when I crossed our finish line...
Like I convinced my brain that you were no longer mine...
But I needed to save face, and you were far behind compared to my pace...
Now I know that we're not in a race, that we both needed some space, but how can I survive without your trace? Without feeling your warm embrace?
Without witnessing your delicacy, your grace?
I've always had a weak memory but how come everything becomes so clear and vivid when it's about you?
Why do I keep on seeing you in every joke, in every talk and in every move?
They say : "Go and date others, they'll help you close the old Chapters", but all I see is your shadow, if it's not this, than what would define a real disaster?
We seemed like two people from different worlds... what are the odds that our energies would match?
I never thought that we'd be a good catch...
I still say this even after we had to end...
I hated commitments until we happened...
I never trusted anyone, and I never was the patient kind...
You made me learn how to love; you made me learn how to match anyone's vibe...
But the deep cut you left is my constant reminder...
I miss you so much, but I have to be wiser.

Although in days like these, I wish that I could be just dumber... or stop being an overthinker...
We're now in April and things between us are way over, but I hate to admit that my love clock stopped back in September...

03.04.2023

Lost and found.

If you ever ask me, when did I find myself, I'll confidently tell you that I'm still looking for my ultimate version to come out to the world.
That same version that confused me for years, depressed me for almost two decades now and held onto past bruises like an abandoned child.
I had to let go of the hatred that filled my heart for the silliest reasons and the scars that inked my body for the most tragic ways of existence.
It looks sparkling for some, very luxurious to others, probably heroic or maybe boring and depriving for a major part. I don't think they're wrong.
I don't think they're right either. I'm all of the above. I've been and still am everything you may love or loathe.
The questioning happens all the time. The unsatisfaction is there to consume the hell out of my life.
This doesn't mean that I'm not grateful for the little details that embellished it or for literally the second chance I was given to pursue certain paths or have some random laughter or have anything I never imagined having.
A very small part of the story was already written and shared with the world, but the story did not reach its end yet.
The story is still going, at least in my brain... But to be realistic, I've done what I believe is right and satisfying.
Albeit I'm not the crazy kind by nature, I did what I think is insane or thrilling enough to distract my brain.

28.06.2023

Re fill

It's like I ran out of words to spill my guts,
and when I do? I know it's time to re fill my cups.
Unfortunately, the costs are quite high, while the revenues are low.
I may be a walking danger that's what I know for sure.
A woman with a little experience in love, doesn't believe in
marriage and won't give you a chance to leave behind some
heritage...
I'm like a player in a soccer field,
and a lover who won't fulfill your needs,
TMI isn't? wait until you read the book,
about my journey as it is.
And how I felt in my 20s.
And the people I had a fallout with,
And the emotions I had to live with.

16.03.2023

That message

I still read that last message I sent you. It was barely a year ago and it was barely a month before you had to be physically gone.
It's still marked as unread. I still wonder if you had the chance to see the things, I said...
Although they were simple, I wanted my few words to be heard. That would make it less painful, that would make our goodbye less absurd.
Your image still appears in my thoughts every now and then, and I know that it's horrible that my thoughts about you aren't that frequent.
But that doesn't mean that you never happened, that you weren't a great man.
and that's why I never wanted to delete our conversation. I wanted to be reminded of you on every occasion.
I want your name to appear whenever I search for someone with your initials.
I want it to be on my contacts' list since you're someone who's truly special.
It would've been nice if you read my book or to see me shine in my newest professional look.
7 is just a number but it was enough to engrave you in my life forever.
If there's ever a universe after this one, I'd love for you to be part of my journey again.

14.04.2023

Relapse

My triggers were always some temporary annoying life events... the kind that come for a short while but leave an unlimited amount of scars deep inside.
and that kind is the easiest to get but it's quite hard to survive.
Despite the endless efforts to go past it, a relapse is unavoidable.
and I'm left with issues that are quite regretful.
My mood swings got me shaking, got me sinking.
which drove me to thinking about the things that I'm hating.
Hating about me, hating in me.
Even if I often just let it be.
Focusing on details that I know would drive me insane.
Not doing activities that I love because of how badly I hate fame.
Not going to a psychiatrist even though I know I need one.
Overwhelming myself for the sake of the fun.
Arguing with hurt people overstaying in any toxic relationship.
Getting angry about their indecisiveness and how they won't let their destiny flip.
Simply giving anyone a chance to diss me for my personality.
Twisting their imperfections around me, which is not the raw reality.
Allowing myself to get angry about stupid topics.
Falling in the trap of logistics.
Getting asked about my opinion for it to be disregarded.
Any chain of emails that are left not responded.
Holding phones when hanging out with friends.
Always putting up my fence.
Women feeling powerless and defeated.

Any person being underestimated.
My very annoying take on food.
Running away from a guy even if he's really good.
Having to explain why I don't want to get married.
Turning a blind eye on the darkness my brain carried.

05.05.2022

Acknowledgement

To all the people who annoyed me, provoked me, angered me, caused some feuds with me, never liked me, or even hated me, I would like to sincerely thank you, not for your actions though, but for the emotions you awakened in me. Without your very generous behaviors, I would not have gone down the path of this artistic journey. Like they say, I was forced to see the bright light through my writing. It was my way to vent, to speak my mind, to release any negativity and to let go of things I believed I should never hold onto.

To all the wonderful creatures who embarked in my world and still stuck around regardless of the moody battles, thank you for letting me squeeze in my vocabulary to also talk about beautiful things and not only the ugly ones.

I might say that reading some of the old things made me cringe at times, and they left me in awe at other times as my feelings were as raw as ever, probably even more mature than my actual age. Regardless of my feelings, I had to leave certain things as they were to demonstrate the reality of things and leave behind a legacy of my past self. It's like a reminder of all the things that should be remembered and all the things that should not.

Poetry, or the slam at this stage, would forever be my biggest source of inspiration, my most cherished talent.

Farah Chamari

About the author

I had officially embarked in my writing path through my first self-published book *"Philia: a journey as it is"*. It was my first personal project as I am currently pursuing a different career.

Writing is one of my biggest passions and hobbies and I do it as a form of healing and growing. It is also a spiritual activity for me as I navigate the world.

"Like a slam" marks my second self-published book, tackling a different genre: Poetry. In fact, I discovered my love for writing through this style and the book was in the making even before the first published one.

Farah Chamari